Published by Gospel Light Publications, Ventura, California 93006

Dedication

To Donna Toberty—a special friend, secretary and co-worker in ministry. Thank you for your years of faithful service. I am deeply grateful for your sacrificial work to bring our ministry to where we are today. You will always be loved and appreciated.

A special thanks to all the students and families in my youth groups over the years whose stories brought me to a deeper faith in Jesus Christ. Sometimes through pain comes freedom.

Acknowledgment

The editors wish to express thanks to Dr. Judy Alexandre for her guidance on some of the case studies contained in this book. Dr. Alexandre is a social psychologist, the director of a Christian counseling center, a speaker, and an active member of Bible Fellowship Church in Ventura, California.

Unless otherwise noted, the standard Bible text is the Holy Bible, *The New International Version.* Copyright © 1973, 1978, 1984 by the International Bible Society. Used by permission of Zondervan Bible Publishers.

Managing Editor, Tom Finley
Youth Editor, Annette Parrish
Assistant Editor, Lauren Ajer
Consulting Editor, Rick Bundschuh
Senior Consulting Editor, Wesley Haystead

Preface

I don't know if I have ever been more excited about a style of teaching and learning than I am with the method of using case studies. A case study is an event or incident that has really happened. Paul Lawrence of the Harvard Business School described a case study as "the vehicle by which a chunk of reality is brought into the classroom to be worked over by the class and the instructor."[1] The greatest benefit of using case studies in Christian Education is that your students will identify with real live people in situations that perhaps relate closely to their own life.

These case studies read like a soap opera but they are all true. Some of them are controversial. Some of the case studies deal with subjects not talked about in the church. But just because we don't talk about sexual abuse doesn't mean there are no sexually abused people in your groups.

Some of the case studies will bring to the surface deep emotions. This is not necessarily bad; we all learn through tension. Life is filled with large and small tragedies; one of the key ingredients of an effective ministry is helping people work through their hurts, doubts, and questions.

Lastly may I say that even though real people are behind every single one of these case studies, some of the names and situations have been changed to protect their privacy.

I would also like to say a special thanks to Rick Bundschuh and Tom Finley, two creative geniuses who challenged me to put this book together. I believe in case studies even more after having completed the project.

Yours in Christ,

Jim Burns
Dana Point, California

1. Marlene LeFever, *Creative Teaching Methods,* (D.C. Cook: Elgin, IL, 1985), p. 240

Table of Contents

PREFACE 3
HOW TO USE CASE STUDIES 6
ABORTION
    Commitment. 9
    Health 10
    Rape. 11
    Values. 12
ALCOHOLISM
    Parental 13
    Teenage. 14
APPEARANCE. 15
CHURCH
    Conflict. 16
    Forgiveness 17
    Group Dynamics. 18
    Lying 19
    Youth Group Situation 20
DEPRESSION 21
DOCTRINE
    Group Dynamics. 22
    Incorrect. 23
DOUBT 24
DRUGS
    Cocaine 25
    Confronting. 26
    Experimentation 27
EATING DISORDERS 28
GOSSIP. 29
HEALTH
    Grief 30
    Loss 31

Ll

HOMOSEXUALITY
  AIDS..32
  Struggle With 33
HONESTY
  Cheating 34
  Lying 35
  Stealing 36
INJUSTICE....................................37
LONELINESS
  Broken Families 38
  Depression 39
LOVE/SEX/DATING 40
MUSIC.......................................41
PARENTS
  Authority 42
  Divorce......................................43
  Friends.......................................44
  Politics.......................................45
  Relationships................................46
PATRIOTISM 47
PEER PRESSURE.............................48
PHYSICAL ABUSE............................49
PRAYER.....................................50
PREJUDICE
  Intercultural Relationships 51
  Response to.................................52
SELF-ESTEEM
  Friends.......................................53
  Unbalanced..................................54
SEXUAL ABUSE
  Incest 55
  Sexual Harassment..........................56
SUICIDE
  Attempted 57
  Cries for Help 58
TERRORISM 59
WAR 60

How to Use Case Studies

Case studies are tools that can bring biblical concepts and principles to life. A case study, as used in this book, is an analysis of an incident from the lives of real people. Questions following a description of an incident guide readers to deal with the difficult situations presented by the study. Students retain more of what they learn because they are involved in the analysis and evaluating process. The case studies in this book are designed to stimulate discussion and interaction in a youth group setting. They might also be used by a group of youth workers to help them work through some of the situations young people face before a teenager comes to them with a similar problem.

The case studies in this book were written to be used in the context of a Bible study. For example in a study of Ephesians 6:1-4, the case study listed under Parents/Friends would give students a chance to practically apply the wisdom in the Scripture to a contemporary, real-life situation. A case study might also be used to open a Bible study; after the group has discussed the case, learners would probably be more interested in investigating what the Bible says about the subject.

Case studies are not meant to be a curriculum. Use them when you want to get an active discussion going on situations relating to your Bible study.

Be sure that you have enough materials and are adequately prepared before class begins. You should bring to class copies of the case study (the pages are perforated for easy removal and you have the publisher's permission to photocopy enough copies for your group), pencils, Bibles, and extra paper. You can customize the case study to fit the needs of your students by adding extra questions or by deleting questions that are not appropriate for your group. Add Scripture references. You may even want to rewrite parts of a case study to draw a closer comparison to your Bible study. Develop the habit of clipping newspaper or magazine articles that relate to the topic you will be investigating. Bring these to class as additional food for thought.

Once in class, be sensitive to group dynamics. You may feel that it is appropriate to separate the boys and girls for some discussions. If you have a large group, you may find that more people will participate in the discussion if you break the large group into smaller groups of four or five. Try to have a group leader in each group. This group leader could be an adult volunteer or he or she could be a student who has demonstrated special ability or who has been discipled for a leadership role. The group leader is responsible for helping to keep the discussion on track and for reporting his or her group's findings or opinions to the class when you reassemble as a large group.

The case study selected for the session is to be read aloud whether in a large or small group. Then the questions should be discussed. A good discussion often has more than one opinion; don't be afraid to let your students agree to disagree.

However, once in a while a group will give totally off-the-mark responses to the questions raised by a case study. While it is not wise to affirm wrong ideas, it is important to allow students an honorable way out of being incorrect. A comment such as, "That certainly is a different answer than I expected," "That view is a common one in our society but let's examine more Scripture to see if it is biblical," or simply, "Thank you for your input. Let's see how another group feels about this question" is much gentler than, "Good grief! Where did you come up with an idea like that?" If you put down a student once, he probably won't share an opinion again and you'll be left in the dark about where he stands spiritually.

Occasionally a case study is loaded with controversy. Even Christians may not agree in every instance. In these cases, allow for differences of opinion, especially in areas where Scripture is silent or subject to several different interpretations. If your denomination has a position on an issue that might be considered controversial, ask your pastor for help in locating the Scriptures upon which your denomination bases its stand.

Be aware that the discussion of some issues, depression, abuse, abortion, alcohol or drug use, may cause troubled kids to open up. You need to be sure that you and the students recognize that a class situation can offer support, love, and prayers for hurting people, but that you *cannot* provide the trained medical or counseling support needed by a person suffering from clinical depression, who has been the victim of rape, or who has a drug dependency problem. Be prepared with suggestions for referral before you use case studies that might help kids open up. Ask your pastor or a social worker to help you formulate a list. This list might include such agencies as Alcoholics Anonymous, Al Anon, a rape crisis bureau, a local department of social services, or a Christian psychologist. Make certain that students who share traumatic experiences are treated with love and dignity. Many people have been put on the road to recovery and healing after confronting their problems in a loving, accepting setting.

Case studies are a good preparation for the jolts of everyday living. They help you and your students be prepared when problems arise. Having been through the thought process, and having investigated the issue in light of Scripture, it is likely that a better decision will be made. The time to decide the right thing to do is before the emotional chaos of a crisis. Using case studies properly will add life to any Bible study and will help guide students to godly decision making. Use of this book can be effective for you, your fellow youth workers, your students, and God's kingdom.

ABORTION

Commitment

Jerry

When Linda told Jerry she was pregnant he was stunned. He felt horrible. He felt responsible and really didn't know what to do. His options weren't very attractive.

You see, Jerry had been waiting for weeks to tell Linda that he didn't love her and that he wanted to break off the relationship. He simply didn't know how to tell her. He had lingered in the relationship because he had felt so guilty about their sexual promiscuity and Linda's dependent, almost helpless attitude toward him. Jerry knew that Linda would probably follow any advice he gave her concerning the pregnancy.

Since Jerry wanted out of the relationship, the easiest thing to suggest was abortion. He could even offer to pay for it. Adoption or keeping the baby would only complicate and confuse the situation.

Jerry's conscience gnawed at him because before this happened he was definitely opposed to abortion. Now he wasn't sure.

1. What would you say to Jerry?

2. Is the Christian answer to marry and try to work out the relationship? Why or why not?

3. What would be Linda's options if Jerry broke off the relationship?

4. What can people do to prevent situations like this one from happening?

ABORTION

Health

Janet

Janet had been living out of wedlock with Tom for two years. She loved Tom very much. The past few weeks Janet had been attending a church where she first became a Christian and then a church member. Tom was not interested in church, but he didn't mind if Janet wanted to go.

One evening after a long talk with her pastor, Janet came home and told Tom, "We either need to get married immediately, or one of us needs to move out." Tom reluctantly chose marriage.

A few months after the wedding Janet became pregnant. A few days after finding out she was pregnant she was told she had cancer. Her doctor advised an abortion.

Janet decided to talk with her pastor about her situation. He suggested that she get a second opinion from a doctor who was a Christian. The second gynecologist said, "If you don't have an abortion, we can't give you chemotherapy. We can't guarantee you'll live for more than two years without chemotherapy."

Tom insisted that Janet get an abortion. Janet was unsure. She sought the advice of more doctors. Five out of seven strongly advised abortion. But Janet decided to carry the baby. She believed God would protect her.

After making this difficult decision, Janet sought out a life-long friend for support, wisdom, and encouragement.

1. How do you feel about Janet's decision to keep the baby?

2. How would you feel if you were Janet? Her husband?

3. If you were the friend Janet turned to, what could you say or do to be a support to her?

4. What do you think is God's part in this whole story?

ABORTION

Rape

Carla

Carla was 25 years old and she was beginning to feel good about her life. She had a good job, a good church, and very supportive friends.

One evening Carla's entire life changed. She was walking in the parking lot of a large suburban mall. It was dark but still busy with traffic. All of a sudden a young man came from nowhere and pulled Carla into a van. He immediately tore at her clothes. She screamed until the assailant hit her in the face and drew blood. He raped her while she quietly whimpered. It all happened so quickly. Then, he drove her to a park, threw her out the back door, and left her in shock, bleeding, and too frightened to move.

An off duty police officer found Carla. He took her to the police station where she told her story. The police officers were kind, caring, considerate, and helpful.

The next day Carla called her pastor. During the next three months, she met with the pastor as well as a trained psychologist who specialized in helping rape assault victims.

One afternoon, crying hysterically, Carla called her pastor. The pastor immediately dropped what he was doing and met with Carla. Carla was pregnant. The only possible father was the rapist. She was literally sick to her stomach. For three months the nightmares brought on by her rape had continued—and now this!

As Carla talked to the pastor, she told him that she felt her only solution was abortion. Although Carla believed that abortion is morally and ethically wrong, she couldn't see another solution. She said, "I cannot carry that baby for six months, even to give it up for adoption. It would kill me!"

1. If you were Carla's pastor, what would you say to her?

2. What are some of Carla's needs?

3. Does rape change the ethics of abortion?

4. What Scripture comes to your mind that might give comfort or guidance to Carla?

ABORTION

Values

Suzanne

Suzanne was 17 and she had a great deal going in her favor. She was a very intelligent and beautiful girl. School work had always been easy for her. Her nearly straight *A* average indicated that she was a perfect candidate for an Ivy League university. She dreamed of becoming a lawyer and politician.

Suzanne was respected by her peers and was sought after as a friend. She had dated several guys from her youth group and church during the past year and a half.

Suzanne began dating a young man she met at church who was in the military. His name was Bob. He was a very nice person who had recently moved to her community from another state. He was lonely and loved the positive atmosphere of Suzanne's circle of friends, church, and home.

A few months after her relationship with Bob became serious, Suzanne came to the office of her youth worker. It was easy to tell that she had been crying for hours. Between sobs she blurted out this story:

> Bob and I went "all the way" once. That month I missed my period but I didn't think much about it. The next month I missed my period and went to a doctor. I am pregnant. I told Bob. He gave me $100 for an abortion and told me that he is transferring away from the area and never wants to see me again. I don't want to tell my family. And I don't want to carry a baby and be a disgrace to all I've stood for. If I keep the baby I'll ruin my chances for going to law school.

Although Suzanne had never been a supporter of abortion, she shared with her youth worker that she had made an appointment to get one in two days.

1. What factors in Suzanne's situation added to her feeling of hurt?

2. Since Suzanne had already made an appointment for an abortion, what might she have been seeking from her youth worker?

3. If you were the youth worker, what would you say? What would you do?

4. In what ways might Suzanne's parents react? How might their reactions affect Suzanne?

5. Read Psalm 139:13-16. How does this passage relate to this case study?

ALCOHOLISM

Parental

Carol

Carol's mother was a very nice woman when she was sober. The only problem was that she was seldom sober. Carol and her family had lived with her mother's drinking habits for years. Her mother would get drunk and become verbally, and at times physically, abusive. There were days when her mother wouldn't come home. Eventually she was fired from her job as a secretary for the school district.

Carol's dad stayed with her mom even though they fought a great deal of the time. But neither Carol nor her dad invited friends to come to their house. They never knew if Mom would be sober.

Carol was beginning to deeply resent her mother. She loved her, but at times felt disgusted by and even hated her. Carol was also angry with her father for allowing her mother to act the way she was acting.

Her mother's drinking was affecting every aspect of Carol's life. She was doing poorly in school. Her anger was turning inward and she began not to take pride in herself. She neglected her appearance. Her mom's alcohol problem was taking a major toll on Carol's life. She felt lost.

1. What active steps could Carol take to deal with the problems caused by her mother's drinking?

2. If you were Carol's friend, what could you do to help?

3. What might help Carol deal with her feelings of anger and resentment?

4. Alcoholism is a family affair. What could the family do to help this situation?

5. What services, counselors, or agencies are there in your area that help the families of alcoholics?

ALCOHOLISM

Teenage

Richard

Richard was a very bright, talented person with a charming personality. Everyone at his school knew Richard and liked him.

At a school assembly on teenage alcoholism, an excellent speaker explained in detail the types of teenage alcoholics and the symptoms of alcoholism. The speaker said that most alcoholics aren't skid row bums but rather are normal people who have a physiological disease. Their bodies become addicted to alcohol. The speaker, who was a recovering alcoholic himself, described cravings for alcohol.

Richard knew exactly what the speaker was talking about because he also had those intense cravings. Richard was beginning to feel uneasy. He suspected that he might fit the alcoholic profile. Some of his friends had even jokingly called him a drunk.

Richard thought to himself, *I'm not an alcoholic, but I'd better quit drinking for a while just to prove to myself that I can.*

The very next week after the assembly Richard found himself craving a drink. He went to his parents' cupboard and took out a bottle. The next thing he was conscious of was waking up in his room. He had passed out.

Richard, along with up to three million other teenagers, is an alcoholic.

1. As a friend of Richard's what could you do to help him?

2. Many people do not realize that alcoholism is a disease. In your group discuss the disease aspects of alcoholism.

3. Where could Richard turn for help?

4. If Richard continued to get worse and yet deny that he had a problem, what if anything could be done to help him?

5. What skilled help for alcoholics is available in your community?

APPEARANCE

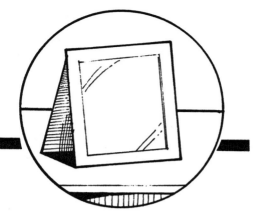

Acceptance

Marie

Marie was a nice person but she was very unattractive. You could tell that she was probably not very encouraged by her looks; she didn't put much time into grooming. Her withdrawn personality was also a hindrance to making many friends. Marie was a very private person.

Although she attended the community church, Marie was not very active or vocal about her faith. Many of the kids in the youth group wanted to make Marie feel accepted by the group but she was a difficult person to get to know. Some of the girls thought they could help Marie look more attractive, but they didn't know how to approach her.

1. How could the girls approach Marie with advice about her looks without hurting her feelings?

2. How could students in the youth group make Marie feel accepted by the group?

3. Do you think there is too much of an emphasis put on looks in our culture? Why or why not?

4. What do you think is God's perspective on physical attraction?

CHURCH

Conflict

The Mission Debate

There was a major debate going on in the youth group. The question was raised "What should the church do with the $250,000 gift from a multimillionaire who had recently died?" The elders of the church had already decided to enlarge the sanctuary to meet the pressing need for more room to accommodate the growing numbers attending the Sunday morning worship.

Many of the youth group members agreed. They thought the large sum of money was God's gift to the church and a sign to enlarge their building. After all, the more people who came to church the more people would be helped. In the long run the enlarged sanctuary would have a very positive impact on the community and eventually the world.

On the other hand, an equal number of the youth group were upset that the money was not going to relieve the life-threatening hunger and shelter needs in Africa. Their reasoning was as impressive as that of the group for enlarging the sanctuary. They kept asking, "What would Jesus do with the money? Would He build a nicer sanctuary or save people's lives?" They cited Bible verses stating the Christian mandate to minister to the poor and oppressed of our world.

The debate was getting intense and the feelings in the room were getting explosive. Both sides were emotional. In fact some young people from both sides were even crying when they pleaded for their position.

Finally the youth pastor stepped in and closed the meeting for the night. Everyone wanted to know his opinion. He didn't tell them. The next day his senior pastor, four elders, and eight parents contacted him to give him their opinion of the youth group meeting.

1. Is this a subject that should have been brought up in the youth group? Why or why not?

2. If you were the youth pastor would you have told the group your opinion?

3. Which side would you have been on in this debate?

4. Do you think there was a right and wrong answer on this subject?

5. What biblical guidelines can you find for handling conflicts?

CHURCH

Forgiveness

Linda

Until recently Linda had been one of the most enthusiastic leaders in the youth group. She didn't miss an event her entire junior year. Her outgoing, charming personality and her servant's heart made her one of the most popular girls in the youth group as well as at her high school.

During the summer between her junior and senior year she became extremely apathetic towards her faith. She began dating a non-Christian boy who was known at the school as a heavy drinker who liked to party. By the time school started rumors were circulating that Linda was partying and sleeping with her boyfriend.

In her junior year Linda had been in the leadership core of the youth group. At the first meeting in September of her senior year Linda showed up as if nothing had happened and wanted to be an active part of the leadership core again.

1. If you were the youth pastor what would you say to Linda?

2. How might the students who had been gossiping about Linda react to her?

3. How might repentance and forgiveness help to heal this situation?

4. Is Linda the only one who needs to ask for forgiveness? If no, who else should take this step?

5. What could have prevented this awkward experience from happening?

6. In 2 Corinthians 6:14,15 Paul advised, "Do not be yoked together with unbelievers. For what do righteousness and wickedness have in common? Or what fellowship can light have with darkness? What harmony is there between Christ and Belial? What does a believer have in common with an unbeliever?"
Do you think this applies to Linda's boyfriend as well?

CHURCH

Group Dynamics

Bob

When Bob was elected student director of his youth group it was one of the happiest days of his life. Since becoming a part of the high school group he had secretly desired to be the student director. He had high goals and big dreams for the group now that he was the student in charge.

The week after his election two mentally retarded teenagers from a nearby home came to the high school Sunday School class attended by most of the group members. It was awkward for many of the students but they all believed it was probably a good thing for Christians to welcome them with open arms. On Wednesday night seven mentally retarded teenagers came to the youth group and it was very uncomfortable. After the youth group meeting several of the regulars complained to Bob about the disruptions caused by the mentally retarded kids. On Sunday nine mentally retarded teenagers came to Sunday School. This time many of the regulars simply said they were not coming back to Sunday School or ever going to bring their friends to youth group meetings until something was done about the problem.

Bob didn't know what to do. He knew Christ loved everyone but the distractions were real. He made an appointment to meet with the youth group leader.

1. What are some options for handling this situation?

2. Whose responsibility is it to find a solution?

3. How do you feel about some of the students saying they wouldn't bring their friends?

4. Do you think the youth group leader should talk to the entire youth group about the "problem?"

18

CHURCH

Lying

Ron

Ron grew up in a strict Christian environment. Although Ron's parents were really nice, they seemed to be overly protective when it came to Ron's social life. Ron was not allowed to go to movies or school dances. In the eyes of his parents many of Ron's friends were not good enough for him.

Ron was not a rebellious person but the attitudes of his strict parents caused him a lot of tension. The only things they wanted him to do were go to church or church youth group activities. But he wanted to do other things as well.

When Ron turned 16 he began to lie to his parents about where he was going. He still was not doing anything wrong in his eyes but more and more he found himself lying about his whereabouts. He would tell his parents he was going to a church activity when actually he was going to the movies with some friends.

Ron complained over and over again to his parents about their strict attitudes but all he ever got from them was, "It's for your own good." Ron began to lie to his parents even more.

1. If Ron was your friend, how could you help him?

2. What difficulties could Ron's lies cause for his youth pastor? What could the youth pastor do?

3. If Ron's mom called you up on the phone and asked if Ron had been at the youth group meeting, what would you tell her?

4. Read Ephesians 6:1-4.

> Children, obey your parents in the Lord, for this is right. "Honor your father and mother"—which is the first commandment with a promise—"that it may go well with you and that you may enjoy long life on the earth."
>
> Fathers, do not exasperate your children; instead, bring them up in the training and instruction of the Lord.

How does this Scripture apply to this case study?

CHURCH

Youth Group Situation

Barry

The youth group at the community church was growing by leaps and bounds. It was exciting to see all of the new kids coming to the group, making decisions for Christ, and getting involved in the church. However, along with the growth there were some problems.

Barry, the young and enthusiastic youth pastor, had been asked to come to the next elders' meeting at the church. The elders all liked Barry and were happy about the exciting youth group. But they did have some questions and problems.

The elders reported to Barry that there had been some complaints. Beer cans had been found in the church parking lot after an outreach concert. Kids ran wild every Tuesday night before and after the youth group meeting. This disturbed the adult meetings at the church. Also, Barry had used up his entire year's budget in only five months. And some parents had complained that the youth group leaders were not mature enough Christians. Lastly there was a deep concern that the church was bringing in undesirables who might potentially steal from the church or draw some of the church kids away from the Lord.

Barry walked out of the meeting disgusted. He immediately wrote up a letter of resignation.

1. Why might the elders have been frustrated by the problems they brought to Barry's attention?

2. Which of their concerns do you feel had the most merit? Why? Which do you feel had the least merit? Why?

3. What options could the church come up with in dealing with the situation in the youth group?

4. If you were in the youth group and heard that Barry had resigned over a conflict with the elders, how would you feel? Would you do anything about the way you felt? What?

20

DEPRESSION

Severe

Christa

Christa was almost always depressed. She usually seemed to be on the edge of tears. Her mother said she was too sensitive. Her father would get mad at her and tell her to quit moping around the house. Christa spent a great deal of her time alone and didn't like to be with her friends anymore. She complained about being tired all the time.

Usually Christa's mom had to force her to get out of bed to get ready for school. While at school Christa spent most of her time alone. After school she came home, closed the door to her room, and did her homework. Then she would spend the rest of the afternoon and evening watching television.

Her mother and father were getting very concerned about the deep, dark depression Christa was apparently experiencing and they made an appointment to meet with their church's youth minister.

1. How might the youth minister help Christa's parents?

2. This is an example of severe depression. It requires professional help. To whom in your area might you refer a severely depressed person?

3. What things do you do to overcome the mild depression that most of us face at one time or another?

4. How can you help friends when they are really feeling low?

DOCTRINE

Group Dynamics

Philip

Philip had been raised in a middle-of-the-road denomination. His church was Bible believing and very evangelical, but conservative in theology. Philip had always gone to church. It was simply a part of his life. He was outspoken on a number of issues, but never caused trouble in the church or at home.

During his junior year in high school, Philip began to attend a Pentecostal Bible study. Speaking in tongues and faith healings were common occurrences at these weekly meetings. Philip began to have a new excitement for the Holy Spirit. It seemed like every conversation he had with anyone at his church centered around the baptism of the Holy Spirit and speaking in tongues.

Philip believed he was called by God to enlighten his church, which he now considered humdrum. He wanted to help them have the power of the Holy Spirit he had found at the Pentecostal Bible study. Philip convinced several of the kids in his youth group to come to the Pentecostal Bible study. Many were baptized in the Spirit and spoke in tongues.

Some of the families at his church were frustrated with Philip. They felt Philip was going against the doctrine of their church.

1. Summarize the situation. What are the facts?

2. Should Philip have left the church he grew up in to attend one whose beliefs were similar to his? Why or why not?

3. Why might the parents of the friends Philip invited to the Pentecostal Bible study be upset?

4. How might the concerned families in the church deal with Philip's enthusiasm for the Holy Spirit?

5. Do you think Philip's actions were divisive or uplifting? Why?

DOCTRINE

Incorrect

Sam

Sam was an intelligent and active member of the youth group. But when it came to Christian doctrine, he was way off base. Many a youth group meeting was spent with the youth leader and Sam arguing over doctrinal matters that no one else knew about, or for that matter cared about.

Almost everyone in the youth group respected Sam's intelligence, but at the same time they got very tired of his debates. Some of the people in the group complained to their youth leader. She confided in them that she really didn't know what to do. Attendance was beginning to drop because people were fed up with the doctrinal debates.

1. What do you think should be done in this situation?

2. How important is correct doctrine?

3. If you were the youth leader, how would you handle Sam?

4. How does Titus 1:9 relate to this study?

DOUBT

Jenny

Jenny wanted to believe as strongly as some of her friends in the youth group. But frankly, she struggled with doubt. When she was honest with herself she acknowledged that oftentimes she even doubted the existence of God. She wondered why she should pray when it seemed like her prayers were bouncing off the ceiling.

Jenny tried hard to muster up faith and to live by faith but she usually fell back to doubting. Sometimes in the middle of church she would think, *What am I doing here? Isn't this a silly make-believe game?* Her mind constantly went over the difficult questions like, *How could a loving God allow so much evil in the world?* and *What about those who have never heard of Jesus? Does God condemn them to hell?*

Finally Jenny made an appointment to meet with a Christian counselor to talk over her doubts and struggles.

1. Is doubting a sin?

2. If you were talking to Jenny, what would you say?

3. Have you ever doubted that God exists? If so, how did you handle your doubts?

4. Many people ask the same questions as Jenny did about evil and those who have never heard about Jesus. How would you answer these questions?

DRUGS

Cocaine

Cocaine Babies

The use of cocaine during a woman's pregnancy is producing an epidemic of infants with visual problems, lack of coordination, developmental retardation and other physical problems. Doctors across the nation report that cocaine babies began to appear about five years ago but have now become commonplace. In Los Angeles they account for more than half of the drug-associated births reported. The users are from all economic classes, and from those who used the drug only once or twice to those who were addicts.

Cocaine's effect on pregnancy is just now becoming clear to doctors. One hospital study shows that "coke" users have a high incidence of miscarriage and a higher-than-normal rate of premature labor. The drug can rob the fetal brain of oxygen or cause the fragile internal vessels to burst, which can leave an infant with permanent physical and mental damage.

After birth, many cocaine babies have experienced week-long states of withdrawal, respiratory and kidney troubles, breathing difficulties, behavioral problems and occasionally death. Officials say the long-term effects are even more serious. As cocaine babies age, doctors are predicting many will experience mental retardation, learning difficulties and problems with simple tasks like eating and dressing.[1]

1. What is your reaction to this article?

2. What can be done to educate people about the use and abuse of drugs?

3. How can you say no when someone you know offers you cocaine?

4. How does 1 Corinthians 6:19,20 relate to this case study?

FOOTNOTE
    1. *Focus on the Family* magazine, June 1986 issue, page 11.

DRUGS

Confronting

Tony

There were very few rules on the church retreat but one of the ones that had been strongly emphasized was that there could be absolutely no drugs or alcohol taken. In fact the retreat information packet stated, "If you are caught with drugs or alcohol you will be sent home immediately."

Tony was new to the group. He was mildly interested in the Christian faith but was known as being a "partier." He confided to a few of his friends that he had hidden some pot and beer in his duffel bag.

After everyone else was asleep, Tony and two of his friends snuck out of their cabin and smoked some pot and drank a few beers. Everyone in the cabin except Tony's counselor knew he had brought pot and beer on the trip. They knew Tony and his friends were sneaking out that first night for a midnight party.

The next day someone told Tony's counselor about the little party. When the counselor confronted him, Tony denied the whole thing and acted hurt that he would even be suspected. When the counselor left Tony was furious. He wanted to find the person who told on him so that he could beat up the snitch.

By now the news of the midnight party was all over camp.

1. Would you have told the counselor about the party if you were in Tony's cabin?

2. Now that the news was all over the camp, what could the leaders do to tackle the problem?

3. What actions could the camp leaders take if Tony and his friends continued to deny that they had been drinking and smoking pot?

4. Do you think that because Tony brought the pot and beer to the retreat he was more to blame than the others involved? Why or why not?

DRUGS

Experimentation

Carmen

When Carmen was 16 he experimented with cocaine. The third time he tried it his parents caught him and confronted him. His response was, "I am only experimenting. Most high school students experiment with drugs, even in the church youth group. I have too high of goals to ever use it repeatedly. And besides, statistics tell us that a majority of medical doctors under 40 use illegal drugs."

His father shouted back, "Those are the silliest excuses I have ever heard! You are not being logical."

1. Statistics tell us that most high school students will at least experiment with drugs. Is this experimentation okay? Why or why not?

2. If you were Carmen's parents, how would you respond to each of his excuses?

3. If you were Carmen's parents, how would you discipline him?

4. Do you think that most Christians experiment with drugs?

5. How do you believe God views drug experimentation?

EATING DISORDERS

Colleen

Colleen was an upper-middle-class girl who was on the drill team at her high school. She was likeable and at times the life of the party. Her parents were both driven workaholics who tended to put a lot of pressure on Colleen to earn good grades and look just right. Her father, whom she adored, at times teased Colleen about acquiring some "love handles" around her mid-section. Colleen wanted to please her parents and wanted to be liked and accepted by her friends.

A friend of Colleen's who was also on the drill team told Colleen about a new form of dieting. She explained in detail how whenever she ate she would either take laxatives or induce vomiting. Her friend claimed that the nutrients got into her body but the calories were flushed down the toilet!

Colleen tried the "diet" and it worked, for a while. But Colleen's small problem of a few extra pounds became a bigger problem. She became obsessed with food. Sometimes she would eat meals large enough for several people. Then she would go into the bathroom and induce vomiting.

After a while her parents noticed a change in Colleen's personality. She seemed to be tired all the time. Her behavior seemed a little weird. One day Colleen's mom read an article in a woman's magazine about eating disorders. The term the magazine used was *bulimia*. That evening Colleen's mom confronted Colleen about her eating habits.

1. Take a moment to summarize this case study. What are the facts?

2. What can be done to help people like Colleen?

3. How can people, especially young women, deal with the emphasis our society places on outward appearances?

GOSSIP

Cindy

Everyone knew Cindy was the biggest gossip in the youth group and maybe in the entire school. How she got all the juicy stories so quickly no one could quite figure out but she usually knew everyone else's business and was never very slow in telling the world.

People talked horribly about Cindy behind her back, but no one had ever confronted her about her gossiping. Frankly, most of Cindy's listeners were eager to hear the latest bit of news about someone else. Cindy had no idea she was known as the church and campus big mouth until one day she accidentally intercepted a note written about her habit of gossiping.

Cindy was devastated by the note. She immediately made an appointment to talk with her youth pastor's wife (who also believed Cindy was a gossip).

1. If you were the youth pastor's wife, what would you say to Cindy?

2. What could her friends have done to help the situation from getting to this point?

3. What do you think is the best way to respond when someone shares gossip with you?

4. Read Proverbs 20:19. What instruction do you get from this verse?

HEALTH

Grief

Jana

Jana had just been told she had cancer. Her doctors wanted to operate within the week. What an experience for a ninth grade cheerleader who was one of the most popular girls in her class! Cancer. Didn't cancer happen to old people—not to vibrant, beautiful, active ninth grade girls?

Jana and her family were extremely active at their church. They immediately called the minister for comfort. They also asked their minister to help them decide if they should allow the doctors to operate on Jana. When the minister heard the story he said that there was basically no option but to operate. Jana and her family decided to go ahead with the surgery.

The operation only brought more bad news. The cancer was so advanced that the doctors gave Jana only six months to live. For most of those months Jana would probably have to be heavily medicated in order to endure the pain.

Jana remained strong in her faith. But her parents' faith wavered. They were bitter and angry at God. Some of Jana's friends in the youth group would come over every day and pray for her. The pain increased. Her faith remained strong as her parents' faith deteriorated. Jana was actually an inspiration to her friends.

Six months from the day of her operation Jana died. There were over 1,000 people at her funeral. It was the saddest of days for all who knew her. Yet Jana's short life had been an inspiration. Along with grief her friends experienced a certain amount of deeply rooted joy and peace. Jana was no longer in pain. She was with the Lord Jesus whom she loved so deeply.

Her parents never set foot in a church again.

1. If you were one of Jana's friends and you knew she had cancer, how would you respond to her?

2. What could the pastor or other friends do to minister to Jana's parents?

3. What steps might Jana's friends take to help them deal with their grief?

4. How would you respond if you knew you were living on limited time?

5. How does this verse make you feel?

   And just as it is appointed for men to die once . . . after that comes judgment.
   Hebrews 9:27 *(RSV)*

HEALTH

Loss

Elizabeth

Elizabeth was a very talented and beautiful person. She was quiet but was genuinely liked and respected by her peers. She had an intense desire to be a growing Christian and her disciplined devotional life was a special part of her life.

When Elizabeth turned 16 her mother convinced her it was time to get a complete physical check-up which included a trip to a gynecologist. Elizabeth was very uncomfortable with the thought of visiting the "female problems" doctor but she gave in to her mother's pressure.

No one ever thought there would be a problem. But Elizabeth's gynecologist did extensive testing and found out that (1) Elizabeth would never be able to have children and (2) she needed to immediately begin taking a hormone supplement. Elizabeth would require this medication for the rest of her life. When Elizabeth heard the news she was devastated.

1. If Elizabeth told you her story what could you do to comfort her?

2. If you were Elizabeth how would you deal with possible feelings of loss?

3. Since Elizabeth had a vibrant faith, how could this experience affect her? (Your response could be positive or negative.)

4. As Elizabeth became older and established serious relationships with men, at what stage in the relationship should she tell them about her inability to bear children?

5. Does the inability to bear children diminish Elizabeth's value as a human being?

HOMOSEXUALITY

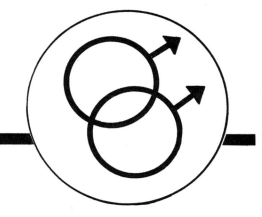

AIDS

AIDS Research

As Christians, we need to consider the questions raised by this article excerpted from *USA TODAY.*

The federal government will spend $100 million over the next five years to test drugs against AIDS, health officials announced Monday.

The money will go to 14 USA medical centers, which will begin testing drugs on about 1,000 patients over the next year. Depending on the results, more patients will be included over the next five years.

But some groups say this testing—measuring a drug against a harmless pill or injection—leaves many dying patients without hope. Congressional hearings on the issue are scheduled for today.

"Taking a sugar pill for a year is not helpful for someone with a year to live," says Lori Behrman of the Gay Men's Health Crisis in New York.

Dr. Mathilde Krim of the American Foundation for AIDS Research says victims shouldn't have to wait for tests.

"The government should make experimental drugs more widely available to AIDS victims," she says.

But Dr. Anthony Fauci, director of the National Institute of Allergy and Infectious Diseases, says, "Some of these drugs can be dangerous and even shorten an AIDS patient's life. It is better to prove that a drug is safe and effective before giving it to everybody."

If testing finds an effective drug, it will be made quickly available, he says.[1]

1. Do you believe the federal government is doing the right thing in investing $100 million to test drugs which possibly will fight against AIDS?

2. Do you believe AIDS is a curse from God on the homosexual population? If yes, how do hemophiliacs who contact AIDS through medication fit into your view?

3. If a friend or family member contacted AIDS, what would you do? How would you feel?

4. What are some fears you might have about AIDS?

FOOTNOTE
   1. Steven Findlay, "USA commits $100M to test AIDS drugs," *USA TODAY,* July 1, 1986.

HOMOSEXUALITY

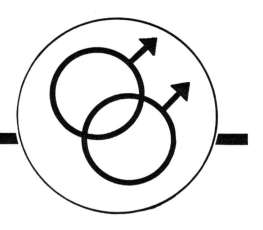

Struggle With

Michael

Michael asked his youth pastor, Spencer, an intriguing question, "What do you think about gay people?" The question came from nowhere and Spencer wondered what Michael was leading to.

Spencer said, "I think gays are people God loves very much but who are extremely confused."

Michael went on, "It really bothers me when the kids in the group are always making fun of gays and doing the limp wrist routine."

Spencer didn't answer the question. Instead he asked Michael a question, "Michael, is this a struggle in your own life?"

It took a long time for Michael to answer but he finally blurted out, "I think so, I'm just not sure!"

1. If you were Spencer, how would you have replied to Michael's statement, "I think so, I'm just not sure!"

2. Do you think Spencer handled the situation properly? Why or why not?

3. If Michael was a practicing gay, should he be allowed to remain in the youth group? Why or why not?

4. How do you feel about Michael's comment that it bothered him when kids in the youth group made fun of gays and did the limp wrist routine?

HONESTY

Cheating

Jeanie's Dilemma

Jeanie was a good student and an active Christian. She was beginning to become good friends with Bill. Bill was a great looking football player who had been showing interest in Jeanie and her church youth group. He sat next to her in math class.

Jeanie knew that a majority of the students cheated on tests. (The National average is 55 percent.) She tried to ignore the problem until one day during a difficult exam Bill asked Jeanie to give him a few of the answers.

1. If you were Jeanie, knowing that Bill was interested in you and becoming interested in the faith, how would you react to his desire to cheat?

2. Is there ever a reason to cheat? Why or why not?

3. What would be your choices of responses if your parents asked you to cheat on a test in order to get a scholarship?

4. Recent statistics tell us that a majority of students in high school cheat. Do you agree with this statistic? On what do you base your opinion?

HONESTY

Lying

Randy

    Randy had a real problem with lying. He probably didn't look at it as lying, just exaggeration. Nevertheless he was known by everyone as one who made up stories or greatly expanded the facts to make them sound more interesting. Many of his lies were centered around making him look better.

    In the small community in which he lived most people said, "Randy is a lot like his dad." Randy's father had some trouble telling the truth. He owed people money and had been deceitful numerous times.

    Randy was active in the community church youth group. He was outgoing, involved, and was contemplating going into the ministry. Many of Randy's friends began seeing less of him because they were bothered by his unbelievable stories. Some of his youth group friends who really loved him made an appointment to talk with their youth pastor to discuss Randy's problem with lying.

1. Do you think the decision made by Randy's friends to talk with their youth pastor will be helpful?

2. If you were the minister what would you suggest his friends do in order to help Randy?

3. Should Randy be confronted about his lying? If no, why not? If yes, how could this be done in a loving, nonjudgmental way?

4. Are self-esteem and lying connected? How?

5. According to Colossians 3:9, what does the Bible say about lying?

HONESTY

Stealing

Carl

Carl was a typical rowdy 13-year-old kid in the church youth group. He was a clown and a goof-off most of the time but sometimes there was a more serious side to him. In fact, underneath his carefully constructed exterior there was a very sensitive young man who tried very hard to impress others.

Carl went on the yearly traditional youth group trip to one of the major amusement parks in the country. He and his buddy were having a great time when all of a sudden the security police stopped them and searched them. Carl's buddy had stolen and stashed in Carl's bag a watch, a hat, and a T-shirt. Carl claimed he knew nothing about the thefts. Carl and his friend spent the rest of the afternoon in the amusement park's police station. Their youth worker was called to the police station over the park's public address system. Both sets of parents were called to come and get their children.

Carl was humiliated. He begged his youth worker not to tell anyone what had happened. When his parents arrived, he claimed innocence. Carl never came back to the youth group.

1. If you were Carl and you were innocent, what could you do to clear your name?

2. What could the youth worker do in this situation to help Carl and his friend?

3. If you were Carl's parents and he continued to plead innocent, what would you do?

4. What could the youth group have done to get Carl to start attending the group again?

INJUSTICE

Jack

In history class Jack was definitely Mr. Murray's favorite student. They joked with each other and during study time in class Jack and Mr. Murray would talk about basketball. You see, Mr. Murray was also Jack's basketball coach. Jack would run errands for Mr. Murray during class that had nothing to do with the history class.

At the end of the first quarter Jack bragged to a number of students in class that he was getting an *A* and that he had only turned in half the assignments. There had only been one exam and Jack received a *C* on that exam.

The other students laughed with Jack, but behind his back they were furious. Why did they have to work so hard to get good grades and Jack goofed off and still got an *A*? It was definitely unfair.

1. Do you think teachers ever play favorites in class? How might this affect other students in the class?

2. As a Christian what, if anything, would you do about this situation?

3. Do you think Jack was doing something unethical? How about the teacher, Mr. Murray?

4. In your own school, what options, if any, would students have for dealing with a situation such as this one?

5. Do Christians need to accept injustice? Support your answer with Scripture.

LONELINESS

Broken Families

Brigette

Steve and his wife saw Brigette coming toward them in the mall two days after Christmas. Steve asked 16-year-old Brigette, "How was your Christmas?" Brigette started to answer, then she broke down and sobbed. Finally Steve put his hand on her arm and said, "Brigette, what's wrong?"

When she finally regained her composure Brigette said, "My mom went out on a date all Christmas Day and my dad never called. I'm so lonely."

1. If you were Steve or his wife how would you respond to Brigette?

2. What feelings besides loneliness might Brigette be experiencing?

3. What steps might Brigette take to make her next holiday a better one?

4. How can the pain of divorced parents cause deep loneliness in a teenager? What can teenagers do about it?

LONELINESS

Depression

Greg

Greg walked into his youth counselor's office with a large tape recorder. He asked if he could play a song for her. He then pushed the button and out blared a song entitled "Lonesome Loser" by the Little River Band. When the song was finished he turned off the recorder and said, "I feel like a lonesome loser."

His statement took the youth counselor by surprise. Greg seemed like a very popular person with lots of friends. When the youth counselor asked about Greg's loneliness, Greg's reply was, "I have lots of acquaintances and no friends." He went on to say, "No one knows the real me. I am desperately lonely. I'm scared at what I might do because I'm so desperately alone. I need help."

1. If you were the youth counselor how would you help Greg?

2. Greg used some of the phrases people say when they are suicidal. This is a serious plea for help. What resources for skilled help are available in your area for people like Greg?

3. This decade has been called the "Decade of Loneliness." Why do you think people describe this generation in this manner?

4. What steps can people take to deal with loneliness?

5. How does the following psalm of David relate to loneliness?

The Lord is my shepherd, I shall not want; he makes me lie down in green pastures. He leads me beside still waters; he restores my soul. He leads me in paths of righteousness for his name's sake.

Even though I walk through the valley of the shadow of death, I fear no evil; for thou art with me; thy rod and thy staff, they comfort me.

Thou preparest a table before me in the presence of my enemies; thou anointest my head with oil, my cup overflows. Surely goodness and mercy shall follow me all the days of my life; and I shall dwell in the house of the Lord forever.

Psalm 23 (RSV)

LOVE/SEX/DATING

Scott and Karen

Karen had recently told Scott that she loved him but didn't want to date anymore. Scott was devastated and begged her to reconsider. Karen remained strong in her conviction that they should break up.

Scott and Karen had been dating for six months. They had really gotten close and in fact in the past two months they had "gone all the way" about eight times. Both of them had been virgins before this. As Christians they both believed it was against their moral standards and the standards of the Bible. But each time they were together they would get carried away emotionally and physically. Later they would feel a tremendous amount of guilt.

Separately and together they had prayed for God's forgiveness and the power to refrain from intercourse. Each time they slipped they felt like they were letting God down. Scott wanted to continue working on the relationship. Karen said the only way out for her was to break up.

1. What options were available to Karen?

2. If you were in Karen's place what would you do?

3. If you were Scott what would you do?

4. Both of these people prayed for help and then slipped. What are your thoughts about this?

5. What kind of advice would you give people in a similar situation as Scott and Karen but who hadn't broken off their relationship?

6. What biblical direction is available to help you face temptation?

MUSIC

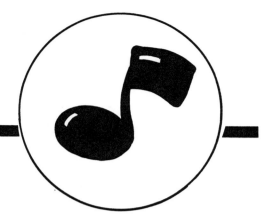

Family Relations

John

In John's own words, "Music is my life." He plays in the school band but his real love is playing the guitar in a local rock and roll band. John doesn't drink or take drugs even though most of his friends do. The harder the rock music the better he likes it.

John is constantly battling with his mother who hates rock music. She thinks most of the stuff John listens to is satanic. She nags him about the life-styles of his friends and the influence it could have on him. She has recently started smelling his breath every time he comes home to see if he has been drinking. John is really getting frustrated.

One evening John had a particularly bad fight with his mom. She said, "If you keep playing that satanic rock and roll you'll have to leave this house." Since John's dad died four years ago, his mom is the head of the household. He loves his mother and he loves his music. He stormed into his bedroom and began to pack his bags.

1. What would you do if you were John?

2. If you were an adult friend of John's mother and she told you this story what suggestions could you give her?

3. If you were a youth pastor and John came to you with this story, what suggestions would you give to him?

4. Does Colossians 3:20 apply to this conflict between John and his mother?

   Children, obey your parents in everything, for this pleases the Lord.

5. Does Ephesians 6:4 have any application in this case?

6. What steps could John and his mother take to reconcile their relationship?

PARENTS

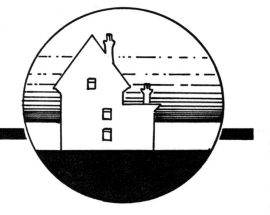

Authority

Katie

Barbara and Katie were really troubled over Katie's parents' decision to not allow them to go on their dream vacation. Ever since Barbara and Katie had become best friends in eighth grade they had planned on going to Hawaii the summer they graduated from high school. Although they never shared their plans with their parents, for a number of years Barbara and Katie had saved money, read up on the Islands, and talked about their dream vacation.

As graduation approached, Barbara's parents were 100 percent behind Barbara taking this special trip. Katie's parents said, "Absolutely not. As long as you live under our roof you won't be taking any vacation alone without adult supervision."

Katie felt that since she was almost 18 and had proven to her parents that she could be responsible, she should be allowed to go. After all, Barbara was not as responsible as she was and her parents thought it was a great idea.

The more Katie wanted to discuss the matter, the stricter and more closed-minded her parents became. Still Katie hoped she could change their minds.

1. Should Katie continue to try to discuss the vacation with her parents? Why or why not?

2. When Katie turns 18 will her options change? How? What circumstances might change your answer?

3. What might be Katie's parents' reasons for keeping her from taking this dream vacation?

PARENTS

Divorce

Todd

In eighth grade Todd's dad wrote a note to him telling him he was going to divorce Todd's mother. His dad was moving to another state. He promised that when things calmed down he would contact Todd and his sister.

Todd felt stunned, hurt, angry, and a hundred other emotions. He knew that his dad and mom had their share of arguments, but divorce was so final. He had many questions. But his mom was so upset she couldn't answer them. In fact his mom had become, in his words, "a basket case."

Three weeks after his dad left Todd still hadn't heard from him. Todd hurt so bad he didn't know who to turn to for help. Then he remembered that one of the youth sponsors at his church had once talked about the pain of divorce. His mom was still a wreck so he decided to talk with Doug, the youth sponsor.

1. What help could Doug offer Todd?

2. What might happen if Todd tried to contact his father?

3. Todd felt angry. What other emotions might a Christian feel in this circumstance?

4. How would you explain this verse to Todd?

   Jesus replied, "Moses permitted you to divorce your wives because your hearts were hard. But it was not this way from the beginning. I tell you that anyone who divorces his wife, except for marital unfaithfulness, and marries another woman commits adultery."

   Matthew 19:8.9

43

PARENTS

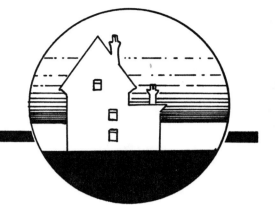

Friends

Lydia

Lydia lived in an Ivy League university town. Her school was made up of upper class kids with extremely high goals. She called these kids "preppies" because a lot of them dressed and acted like prep school kids.

Lydia's parents both worked for the university and hoped that someday Lydia would attend an excellent university and become a successful lawyer or business person.

Lydia's real interest was art. She loved to wear what her parents termed "weird" clothes. She thought most of her "preppie" acquaintances were snobs; she just didn't fit in with that crowd.

Lydia's parents fought daily with her over the clothes she wore, the artsy friends she spent time with, and her apparent lack of motivation to succeed in school.

1. What was Lydia's problem?

2. What was her parents' problem?

3. While Lydia lived at home, how might she handle her parents' wishes concerning her dress, friends, and school work?

4. What could have been done to prevent daily arguing between Lydia and her parents?

5. Can you think of any ways both Lydia and her parents could have compromised a little?

6. Read Ephesians 6:1-4. How might this Scripture be applied to Lydia's situation?

PARENTS

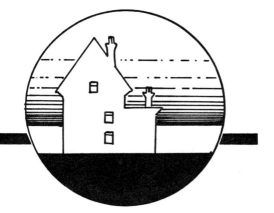

Politics

Stephen

During Stephen's senior year in high school he began to spend time with a number of friends who were very politically active. Stephen had grown up in a home that was very conservative politically. His new friends were quite liberal.

Stephen's friends convinced him that Christians should provide sanctuaries for the thousands of illegal aliens who came into their country every month. His friends said God called Christians to help the poor and oppressed. They showed him Scripture after Scripture to support their point.

Stephen began to work every weekend in the basement of a church that was providing food and shelter for men, women, and children who had entered his country illegally. Stephen realized that what he was doing was a criminal offense. If caught he could be sent to prison. But he was also convinced that he was doing the will of God.

In April of his senior year Stephen's parents found out what he was doing and forbade him to ever work with illegal aliens again. They showed Stephen Scriptures that challenged him to obey his country's laws and to obey his parents.

Stephen found the whole situation very confusing.

1. Summarize Stephen's dilemma.

2. Should Christians, in an attempt to better follow God's will, ever disobey the law of the land? Support your viewpoint with Scripture.

3. Is it possible for two strong Christians to have opposing political views and still be in the will of God? Explain your answer.

4. Does Romans 13:1,2 relate to this story? How? What about Proverbs 28:27? Acts 4:19?

PARENTS

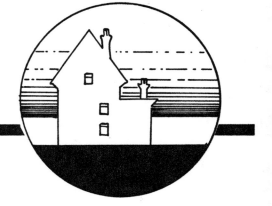

Relationships

Charlene

Charlene had always felt there was something missing in her life but she could never get a handle on what it was. After all, she came from a good Christian home where her parents would soon be celebrating their twenty-fifth wedding anniversary. She had plenty of money, a good church, and a positive school environment.

One day she read an article which stated that fathers spend an average of eight to twelve minutes a day with their children. The statistics caught her eye. Her first reaction was to feel pity for all who had it so bad. Then she realized that over a period of a week she seldom even spent that amount of time with her father. She loved him but she realized she really didn't have much of a relationship with him. He worked long hours and when he wasn't working he was watching sports on television or reading the newspaper. When he came home he would say "Hi" to all the kids. Charlene realized she and her dad had not spent any time together for years. She felt empty. She felt a deep void in her life.

That night after dinner she sheepishly approached her father to talk about her concern.

1. If you were Charlene, what would you have said to your dad?

2. Do you suppose there are many people who feel as Charlene feels?

3. What are some practical suggestions that might help Charlene and her dad build a better relationship?

4. What can you do to make your relationship better with your family?

5. If you were a parent, what could you do to make sure that you spent meaningful time with your son or daughter?

PATRIOTISM

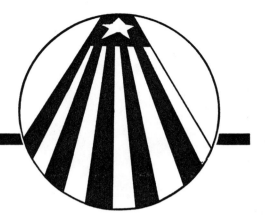

The following is an article from *USA TODAY*. It contains some interesting information on the topic of patriotism.

Forty-three percent of USA adults think we're more patriotic than 10 years ago, says a *USA TODAY* poll.

Only 24 percent of 1,000 randomly selected adults think we're less patriotic. Thirty percent see no change.

Fifty-two percent feel as patriotic as they did a decade ago; 39 percent feel more patriotic.

"Many of us from the babyboomer years are starting to realize you pay a price for freedom, and when you pay a price you realize how patriotic you need to be," said David W. Reng, 39, of Newport, Wash.

Recent terrorist actions, said Francis Einig, 45, of St. Louis, "evoke different feelings, patriotic feelings."

Fifty-four percent think the founding fathers would be proud of us; 38 percent said they'd be disappointed.[1]

1. Is patriotism a Christian attitude? Why or why not?

2. What would your feelings be if a friend said he loved his country, but would not fight or join the Army because of his religious beliefs?

3. Why do you suppose people are more patriotic today than they were 10 years ago?

4. In what ways could patriotism compete with Christianity?

5. In what ways might patriotism complement Christianity?

FOOTNOTE
1. Cheryl Mattox Berry, "Patriotism on the rise, poll finds," *USA TODAY*.

PEER PRESSURE

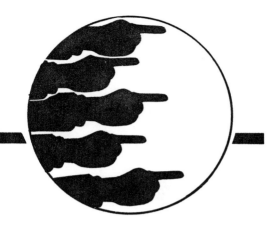

Stealing

Patty

Patty had always been a really good person. Of her three brothers and two sisters she was the one who got in the least trouble. Her parents always praised her and said they believed Patty had a bright future.

Patty had never stolen anything in her life. But her friend Nancy convinced her that it would be easy to steal a swimsuit. All she had to do was put it under her clothes and walk out of the store. Patty felt really torn between her moral convictions and her desire to be accepted by Nancy as one of the gang. She decided to steal the swimsuit just this one time. She put her clothes on over the swimsuit. When she got to the door of the department store, a store detective caught her.

Patty was horrified; she was embarrassed. It was the worst day of her life. Nancy was already out of the store and had gotten away with her theft. The detective took Patty into a back office and treated her like a common criminal. He did say, however, that he would not call the police but would call her parents instead.

Patty sat quietly. She was numb. She wanted to vomit but couldn't move.

When the detective called her parents he had to get tough in order to convince them that it was Patty who had been caught red-handed stealing. Patty was afraid and ashamed when her mom and dad came into the office. They were angry.

On the way home from the store Patty's parents yelled at her and put her on restriction for six months. Patty went straight to her room and sobbed. She knew in her heart she would never steal again.

1. If you were Patty's parents, what kind of punishment would you have given her?

2. What makes peer pressure such a strong influence in a young person's life?

3. Do you think Patty should talk to Nancy? If yes, what should she say? If no, why?

4. How might Patty's parents respond to her differently following this incident?

PHYSICAL ABUSE

Violence

Ashley

Ashley was normally an outgoing, energetic person but at the youth group pool party she sat quietly and watched. She had her swimsuit on underneath her sweatshirt and pants, but was the only one not in the pool on this warm July evening. Many of the kids had tried to get her to join in their fun, but it was no use.

Cathy, the youth pastor's wife, very perceptively asked Ashley to help with the preparation of the food. Ashley jumped at the chance. Cathy tried to talk with Ashley, but Ashley did not seem to want to discuss what was bothering her and remained extremely quiet.

One of the mothers said someone would need to go to the store to buy more ice. Cathy volunteered, "Ashley and I will make a store run."

In the car Cathy tried to make small talk but Ashley remained quiet. On the way back from the market Cathy finally blurted out, "What's wrong, Ashley? Has something happened to you?"

Ashley's eyes welled up with tears and then she began to sob. Ashley confided to Cathy that her father had beaten her up pretty badly and she couldn't go swimming because of all of her bruises. Ashley continued to tell her story to Cathy in the car. She seemed grateful to have someone to talk to.

1. After Ashley was through talking, what might Cathy do to comfort and help her?

2. Ashley was a victim of physical abuse. What could she do to receive help?

3. If you were Ashley and you had been physically abused, how would you feel? Where could you go for help?

Note: In some states it is illegal to withhold information about child abuse from the authorities. You should know the laws of your particular location.

PRAYER

God's Sovereignty

The Faith Healer

Sixteen-year-old Karen was lying in a coma in the community hospital. She had been in a horrible accident and was still on the critical list. But the doctors had not given up hope.

The same week that Karen was in the accident, her church was having an evangelistic crusade. The guest speaker was an evangelist and faith healer. The pastor of the church and Karen's parents asked the faith healer to come to the hospital to pray that Karen's health might be restored. He agreed to try.

They all went to Karen's hospital room where she was literally being kept alive by a machine. The faith healer prayed and in a very excitable voice claimed that God had healed Karen.

Her parents were ecstatic and the pastor cried tears of joy. Karen remained in a coma. The faith healer insisted that she had been healed and that as a demonstration of faith they should ask the doctors to disconnect the life support machine.

The doctors and nurses disagreed. Karen's parents went to court to get an order to force the hospital to disconnect the machine. Eventually Karen was taken off the machine at the insistence of the family and a court of law.

Karen died three days later.

1. What is your impression of this true story?

2. If you were Karen's parent or pastor, how would you feel?

3. Did God not answer the faith healer's prayer?

4. Have you ever prayed for something and it didn't turn out as you wished? What was it?

5. Do you think God heals some people and chooses not to heal others? If yes, explain why you think God does this. If no, explain the problem posed in the story of the faith healer.

6. Read Matthew 21:22 and 1 John 5:14,15. How do these verses relate to this case study?

PREJUDICE

Intercultural Relationships

Antonio

Antonio's parents were both born in Mexico. For a number of years they had lived and worked illegally in Los Angeles. At home Antonio spoke Spanish; at school he spoke English.

Antonio was an extremely bright student who maintained an A average. He was the most valuable player on the school's football team and on the baseball team. He was active in school government and was even elected most likely to succeed. Antonio was the pride and joy of his parents and his school.

During the end of his senior year, Antonio became close friends with an Anglo girl who was also very intelligent and talented. They eventually became boyfriend and girlfriend. She started bringing him to her church. Antonio was very interested and excited about what he was learning at the church.

One day his girlfriend met him in a heap of tears. Through the sobs she said that her parents had forbidden her to see him any more because he was Mexican. Her parents had talked with the pastor and she said the pastor agreed that the relationship should be broken off.

Antonio was stunned. His girlfriend was in shock and they didn't know what to do or say.

1. How do you feel about this situation?

2. What potential challenges are presented by an intercultural or interracial relationship or marriage?

3. Why might the parents and pastor have wanted to force Antonio and his girlfriend to break up?

4. How do you think God would view this situation?

PREJUDICE

Response to

Larry

   The first 10 years of Larry's life were spent in the ghetto. Like many young black people, Larry didn't know many white kids and his thoughts and feelings were mixed when it came to racism.
   When Larry was 11 years old his mom remarried a businessman who lived in an upper-middle-class suburb where most of the kids were either white or oriental. There was only one other black at his school.
   Most of the kids at school were very friendly and the teachers were great. Yet there were a few kids who were rude to Larry. They would write little notes on his locker calling him a nigger and telling him to go back to the ghetto.
   As a Christian, Larry wanted to love everyone. But all the ridicule was getting to him. His frustration and disgust toward some of the racist kids in his school was growing. And although Larry didn't believe it was right, he was beginning to hate the racists.
   His mother, stepfather, and he made an appointment to speak with the school principal.

1. How does ridicule and rejection affect a person?

2. What Bible verses might help Larry deal with this situation and with his feelings?

3. If you were a friend of Larry's, what could you do to help him?

4. How could the school principal help?

5. What do you think makes some people more prejudiced than others?

SELF-ESTEEM

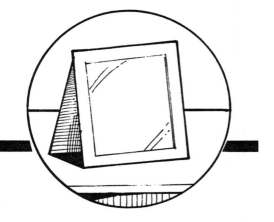

Friends

Clint

Clint was very unsure of himself. He was the smallest kid in the class and he had been in nine schools in 12 years. His father was in the armed forces and their family moved almost every year.

Clint was quiet and reserved. It was very difficult for him to make friends because he didn't want to get close only to experience the pain of another move.

In one of Clint's really low moments, he came to his school counselor and poured out his heart. "I'm short and I hate being short. I don't have any friends. I hate moving and it looks like we'll have to move again next year."

1. If you were Clint, what would you need or want to hear?

2. What could Clint do to help make the best of his situation?

3. What could Clint's parents do to help his situation?

4. If you were his acquaintance, what could you do to help Clint?

SELF-ESTEEM

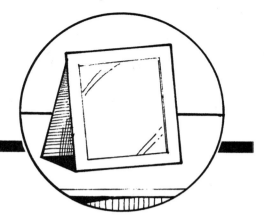

Unbalanced

Nicki

Nicki always put herself down. Even when someone tried to compliment her about her hairstyle or clothes she wouldn't accept the compliment at face value. She also tended to be a complainer. Deep down inside she hated herself and knew she was becoming a very negative person.

Nicki's parents constantly nagged her not to be so critical of herself. Yet she couldn't get the negative thoughts out of her head. Nicki didn't like her looks; she hated her clothes. She felt that if she were taller she would be prettier. Nicki even hated her quiet personality. There were times when she even resented God for not making her a different person.

1. If you could tell Nicki anything, what would it be?

2. How can you build a healthy, well-balanced self-esteem?

3. How does Psalm 139:13-16 relate to the concept of self-esteem?

   For you created my inmost being; you knit me together in my mother's womb. I praise you because I am fearfully and wonderfully made; your works are wonderful, I know that full well. My frame was not hidden from you when I was made in the secret place. When I was woven together in the depths of the earth, your eyes saw my unformed body. All the days ordained for me were written in your book before one of them came to be.

4. What step could Nicki take to build her self-esteem?

SEXUAL ABUSE

Incest

Monica

When Monica was nine years old her older brother molested her. It was a terrible, traumatic experience which she told to no one because her 14-year-old brother threatened to kill her if she told. The next month her brother raped her. For the next two and a half years he had sexual relations with her, always vowing to kill her if she told anyone.

Monica never told a soul. Her brother was a violent person and she feared for her life. She withdrew. She flunked most of her classes and experimented with drugs given to her by her brother. Finally her brother was arrested for armed robbery and Monica was free of the horror of more traumatic experiences.

An acquaintance of Monica's invited her to a weekend retreat at a Christian camp. There for the first time in her life she heard about God's unconditional love for her through Jesus Christ. She wanted to become a Christian, but her haunting past experiences kept her from coming to Christ.

After coming home from camp she made an appointment with a youth pastor and told him her story.

1. What are some signs of sexual abuse?

2. If you were the youth pastor, what would you do or say to help Monica?

3. How could you help others who have been victims of sexual abuse?

4. What can Christians do to help prevent the horrors of sexual abuse?

5. In your community, to whom would you refer a victim of sexual abuse for expert help?

SEXUAL ABUSE

Sexual Harassment

Bonnie

Bonnie was baby-sitting at her ex-boyfriend Tom's house. She was very close to his little sister and his family even though Tom and she had broken up. Tom's stepfather had always been very nice to Bonnie. In fact she often wished she had a father as special as Tom's stepfather.

Tom's family was going out to dinner and to a play while Bonnie watched the youngest child. Tom's stepfather, Ted, would be home but he would be working in the back room.

The moment Bonnie put the little girl to bed Ted came into the kitchen and asked Bonnie if she wanted some popcorn. Bonnie loved popcorn and said, "Thanks. That will be a good addition to the program I'm watching on television."

Ted made the popcorn then sat down on the couch next to Bonnie and started watching the program with her. Bonnie complained about a sore back which she had gotten from playing softball. So Tom's stepfather began to rub her back. At first he rubbed outside her sweater, but after a while moved his hands under her sweater.

Bonnie froze. She didn't know what to do. She didn't know if this nice man was going to go farther or was just doing her an innocent favor. Bonnie was tense and nervous. In a soft voice Tom's stepfather told her to relax; it would be better for her backache.

The phone rang. Bonnie was grateful for the distraction. Tom's stepfather, reluctantly it seemed, got up to answer the phone.

1. If you were Bonnie what would you do?

2. Do you think it was okay to baby-sit while the stepfather was still home? Why or why not?

3. If you were Bonnie's youth pastor and she told you this story, what would you say or do?

4. If you were Bonnie, would you tell Tom or his mother about this incident? Why or why not?

SUICIDE

Attempted

Tina

Tina was one of the leaders in her church youth group. She was outgoing, friendly, and respected by her peers. Her father and mother had recently separated in what had the potential of becoming a very messy divorce. Tina's younger brother and sister had lots of problems, but Tina seemed to have it all together. If this separation and pressure at home bothered her, she sure didn't show it.

Tina's boyfriend had recently broken up with her. But even when she talked to others about that situation, she really seemed to have a good perspective.

Everyone was shocked when they heard she was in the hospital because she attempted suicide.

1. What made Tina's attempted suicide even more surprising?

2. What could Tina have done to get some help before her attempt to take her own life?

3. What could some of Tina's friends have done to help her when her family separated and her boyfriend dropped her?

4. In your community, to whom could you refer a person who was suicidal so that he or she could get expert help?

SUICIDE

Cries for Help

Debbie

The call came shortly after midnight. Tammy was in a pay phone booth saying, "I'm sorry to wake you up, but Debbie says she is going to kill herself and I think she is serious. Can we come over?"

"Of course," Jim replied.

Within 10 minutes Debbie, Tammy, and Jim were sipping hot coffee and listening to Debbie's story. Debbie's boyfriend had been cheating on her, and the other girl was her best friend. Her mother had recently left her second husband and was drinking heavily. She had violently struck out at Debbie that day. Debbie was failing four of her six classes. She couldn't sleep over two hours at a time. She was deeply depressed.

Two years before, Debbie had slit her wrists and was found unconscious. The doctors who treated her following this suicide attempt had said that she would have died within 15 minutes if she had not been rushed to the hospital. Jim and Tammy believed Debbie would try it again.

1. If you were Jim or Tammy, what would you do to help Debbie?

2. This is an example of a life-threatening situation that calls for expert help. To whom would you refer Debbie for this help?

3. If you were Tammy or Jim, would you call Debbie's mother?

4. What do you think God thinks of suicide?

5. What are the signs of a person being suicidal?

TERRORISM

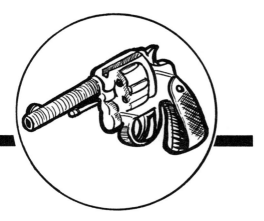

Laurie

Terrorism is a very frightening aspect of our world today. With the increase of terrorist activities all over the world, traveling has become more of a risk.

Laurie and her family were planning a trip to Rome, Italy. They had worked, dreamed, and saved for this trip for five years.

Two months before the trip 16-year-old Laurie informed her parents that she was not going to Italy. Yes, she had been as excited as anyone else to go, but now she feared for her life and for the lives of the other members of her family. Laurie said that she would never be able to enjoy her trip because of her constant fear of a terrorist attack.

Laurie begged her parents to reconsider. "Let's put this trip off another year or go someplace safe," was her suggestion.

Laurie's father, mother, and older brother all felt her fears were unjustified and strongly believed that they should go to Rome as planned. They teased Laurie for being overly cautious and tried to calm her by saying when she got to Europe she would have the time of her life.

But Laurie remained very fearful. The conversation around the dinner table began to center around Laurie saying that she was not going to Italy and her parents replying that they expected her to get on the plane, fly to Rome, and enjoy herself.

1. Do you believe that Laurie's fears were well-founded? Why or why not?

2. What options did Laurie's parents have in responding to her fears? Which do you believe is the best option?

3. What can be done to combat terrorism in the world?

4. Should one government retaliate against another that is known to be sponsoring terrorist activity?

WAR

Dan

If there was one thing Dan was adamant about it was his view that war is wrong. Dan's father was killed in the Vietnam War. Dan saw that war is a fiasco. He was always telling anyone who would listen, "We (the United States) should never have been in Vietnam. Thousands of Americans like my dad died for no reason at all." He was aware that other people's opinions about Vietnam differed, but Dan continued to persist. He felt that his calling from God was to try to stop future wars.

As a Christian, Dan opposed any military buildup or any military action toward another country. He quoted a host of Scriptures to back his view.

Dan felt it was his *Christian duty* to speak out against the United States' involvement in Central America. He believed it would turn into another Vietnam. He always joined in marches to protest his government's position.

Dan met regularly with his youth pastor and others in his church who didn't share his view on war. In fact, the church he chose to attend was conservative theologically and politically. Dan felt it was his calling from God to inform and persuade his church to become more politically aware of the wrongness of war. Dan was a pacifist and believed Jesus would have been also.

One day as tension mounted in Central America, Dan came to the church youth group with anti-war pamphlets and a paper he had put together with 24 Scripture verses. The handouts stated why war was wrong in the sight of God. The youth pastor wouldn't let Dan pass out the pamphlets or the paper with the Scripture verses.

1. How might the loss of his father have affected Dan's beliefs?

2. Do you believe there is a *Christian* view on war?

3. Do you think it was God's calling for Dan to be so dogmatic about his position? Why or why not?

4. What is the role of Christianity in politics?

5. Do you believe the youth pastor should have allowed Dan the opportunity to pass out his pamphlet and Scripture verses? Why or why not?